Eternal Fascination

Water turned into wine

Miree Ban

authorHOUSE®

AuthorHouse™
1663 Liberty Drive
Bloomington, IN 47403
www.authorhouse.com
Phone: 1-800-839-8640

First published by AuthorHouse 4/29/2010

ISBN: 978-1-4520-1740-2 (e)
ISBN: 978-1-4520-1738-9 (sc)
ISBN: 978-1-4520-1739-6 (hc)

Library of Congress Control Number: 2010905792

Printed in the United States of America

Bloomington, Indiana
This book is printed on acid-free paper.

Eternal Fascination

Prologue

Desire of my soul,

It's a whole new life.
His grand and amazing love, there is
Nothing I can compare it to,
Nothing I would change it to.

This is my testimony poem.

Though my life is
So very plain and ordinary,
Not a successful one in this world,

There is love that enlightens my ignorance,
Carefully touching deep inside my heart;

I sing this song of my new soul.

Realizing purpose and love in Jesus in my ordinary days,
I devote this simple lyric with thanks and blessings.

I'm not adequate enough to write anything like poetry,
But this work is a natural thanksgiving for His
guidance and companionship in life.
Here I dedicate this "Natural flow of heart" to God.

Trusting his constant, caring hands during hard times,
Let my widely roaring self be dead
And my sickening innermost be burnt every day
So that his love and peace will be able to reach others.

A spiritual battle against destiny will
Change our negative and weak personalities.
We are strong enough to beat the evils that threaten us

Whenever we're praying;
He strengthens our minds and becomes our power,
Carried away with love
We can overcome any difficulties and
Not be shaken by the world's allures.

The love I met in the middle of the storm is now blazing.
The more that I crash into, the stronger and wiser I become with it.
Without fears, but with a firm faith,
I live a mature Christian life, day by day.

I hope we experience God's love together,
And adore him more in comfort.
He, who became a victory, is true to us
When we suffer from different kinds of problems.
And I also expect that this song of the cross
and of love will be sympathized with.

In hardship and suffering,
We, His people, surrender to Him,
Giving thanks to Jesus, who is love.

So let's walk along in courage and hope,
Make our dreams come true, and be full of grace.
That is my prayer for you.

Because with faith there is a Heaven's banquet,
A whole new life,
And real joy for those who love the Gospel.

And it is His hope that we're free from sin,
Stay at peace, and dwell in our love for the world.

Let us praise the Lord who is the Creator;
Release all personal, domestic, and social concerns;
And let the name of Jesus be known.

Miree Ban

"Attached to the article published poet, poetry Miree Ban"

As I was reading these poems
In dark and long times, watching the stars,
And thinking of the difficulties of living,
I watched a ray of light
As dear as diamonds and as pure as pearls. I read
In it the same faith, love, and hope.

The poet
Couldn't bury the rays in darkness,
In the sparkles of his life, in that
Painfully dark and hopeless reality.
He began to pray to endless
God, in pure rays of light.

This poet took this life,
The long pain and tests
Found in its deeply buried realities, and polished them to shine,
Like beautifully blooming flowers, or
With the clarity of diamonds, he filled it with "life's words."

This poem is to be read after night has passed
and before the sun rises at dawn.
It gives hope like the hope found in the sight of a new day.

This poem should be read in the depths of night,
In the night when sleep is lost, so that time stands still in endlessness.
It leads me into the depths of God's embrace.

This poem should be read during dangerous, perilous times.
It will give sight to those that are lost from
being exposed to too bright a light.
Also, hearing will be returned to those who have lost
it because of the noise of useless speeches.

Deeply hidden,
Lost love
In lost time is
Like being helped to a cool drink while lost
in the depths of a mountain.
These poems are
Deeply engrained, desperation's salvation from
emptiness. They give off light as life finds its song.
Before dawn's first light, the early morning's sky is without stars.
There are darker times here, darker than the deepest darkness, and you
Wait throughout endless night for the dawn's early light

While withstanding the deep night, the soul falls asleep, lonely, tired.
In that time, the dawn's only star,
Like the soul's confession, withstands the long night.
The dawn's light is gaining hope through this song.

Faith is like the poet's life, that grinds and
polishes diamonds and pearls,
Able to see the clean and great beauty in them.

This poem sings of love.
This poem sings of faith.
This poem sings of hope.

Rev. Joongurn Kim, Pastor
The First Methodist Church of Flushing

Recommendations of the words

Flower that is made of suffering,
Cross that is made of the suffering of Christ:
There is life,
Also, spirit.
It is not glorious, but there is truth.
If one sees beauty once, one wants to keep
it by one's side, to see it often.
Even in the worst circumstances, one looks to light and blossoms,
Beautiful and all encompassing.

Never-changing fascination is kept within this poem.
Representing God and Jesus Christ's meeting with us
As leader of this greatness.
Instead of feelings coming easily,
One can read again and understand
Within one's own life, can witness a
Beautiful soul's fragrance
In the endless trail approaching faith in God.
Suffering and testing are brought about by deep trials.
Love and hope and faith are sung as valuable songs.
Prayer makes us realize that we are alive.

Suddenly, I realize that I am part of the poem and
I am taken hold of strongly by the poem.

In this poem is Jacob's prayer,
Job's faith,
David's consistency,
Esther's courage,
And the wisdom of those who went with Christ.

Difficult and strenuous, life is like a changing wave.
After recognizing the words written here and the mind behind them,
I wish that it is not hopelessness but a true wish that helps you find
Your way through life.

I am giving thanks to God.
He has allowed me to understand Christians' lives.
I also had Christ's guidance for each word,
And I give thanks to the poet.

Moreover, to those Christians who held
This book and followed God's guidance,
And to their brothers, sisters, and readers:
Congratulations on having received the
Guidance of the Lord in doing so.

Rev. Jongsoo Kim, Pastor
The Baptist Church of God

Dear Readers:

I hope you will enjoy reading Miree Ban's delightful poetry as much as I did.

I am delighted to write to you on behalf of Miree Ban, a highly promising poet who is desirous of having her work published.

I am intimately acquainted with Miree and her family's leadership in the Korean American community and with their contributions to the community I represent.

Miree's poetry embodies the unique perspective of her faith and heritage, expressing her devout religious convictions and spiritual passion. Her utilization of rich, evocative language and vivid imagery makes her work truly a pleasure to read.

In view of the above, I respectfully request that you make every effort to publish Miree's poems, so a wider audience can enjoy the fruits of her prodigious labor and talent, which affords one the opportunity to view our world in a thoroughly inspiring light.

Sincerely,

Frank Padavan
New York State Senator, 11th District
Vice President, Pro Tempore

Eternal Fascination

Prologue v

1). He is my perfect father
    1. Shepherd 3
    2. Ancestors were relieved 5
    3. Love..9
    4. Be a tall tree 12
    5. Sailing..15

2). Water turned into wine
    1. Water turned into wine.....................................19
    2. Faith from conception 23
    3. Holiness 26
    4. The Cross 28
    5. Dove of Holy Spirit..30

3). Truly, truly
    1. Truly Truly 33
    2. Mother 38
    3. Wilderness..41
    4. In front of the Lord..43
    5. New Jerusalem 45

4). Overcoat
    1. Overcoat..49
    2. Yoke...52
    3. Test 53
    4. Reconciliation...55
    5. Blessing..57

5). The narrow road
    The narrow road..61

6). Thorn Bush Love
    1. Thorn Bush Love..73

 2. New Sky and New Earth...76

 3. Resurrection 78

 4. Recognition of the Soul...79

7). Poppy

 1. Poppy...83

 2. Sea..85

 3. Beautiful Temptation 86

 4. To love is...87

When we just wait and wait, wander **90**

Our Lord, who built and shared a statue of faith, gave power to His only begotten son, to save and accompany all believers, who changed to meet His character, destructed evils upon demand, showed a new vision, and kept creating and showing the way to accomplish His dream

1). He is my perfect father

1. Shepherd 1 2
2. Ancestors were relieved 1 2 3 4 5
3. Love 1 2 3
4. Be a tall tree 1 2 3 4
5. Sailing 1 2

He is my perfect father.

Shepherd

1

Love that flows
Over the words to the body

Becomes a sword,
Running through Heaven's river.

Fresh raindrops
Soak into the ground,

A miracle of living water,
Open to anybody who is willing.

Soft and clear sounds
Spread to heaven and earth;

Wake up to the light of the world!

Whisper in the presence of Jesus;
How deep and amazing is His love.

2

Long ago, I was reborn,
With a humble and adoring soul.

His love, His smile,
They flow in me still.

Oh, the caring He has for His lambs:
It's a beauty of hugs and kisses to the soul.

He has praise and admiration
For the poor in humble places,

But he cherishes them more
And lets them know He is pleased.

Oh, He's the greatest shepherd,
Leading us to green grass, stream waters.

☆ What is Prayer?
A road with no end. A broad road where you can meet God, an operating room that clears filthy intestines and dirty brains, an onion that reveals secrets as it is peeled, the vision of achieving his creation, a water tank that holds the water of life, a telescope that can see his will, a house of rest where you can ask questions, a changing highway that resembles God by dying and then rising every day.

Ancestors were relieved

Mental illness—
It is too early to see how temporary life is.

Unblooming,
To live is like idling
In an unrealistic daydream.

Each day repeats, the same,
And even breathing gets harder.

Endlessly weighing thoughts
While moaning true confessions:

Examine yourself as if through a microscope,
And it shows symptoms of your self-torture.

Repeatedly, you chew darkness
In a stifling and isolated life,
Confined in a square frame,
Like birds singing sadly.

Vaguely,
Longing for an unknown world,
A sad soul dreaming of hope.

2

Cling to an invisible world
While hope awakens the soul.

You cannot live like a coward.
The best way forward is to follow your gut,
And I risked my life

Waiting for earnest help,
Asking for an ideal world with all my might,

Filling my empty stomach with spirit,
And daring myself to experience things and live fully.
But every measure was insufficient,
And it is an obviously incomplete life:
You cannot escape such a small bird cage.

Looking for worthless things,
Thinking of death becomes disgusting.

That which was not a song
Emerged here and there.

Seeing your detestable self
And accusing yourself of your sickening sins
Brings you closer in your meeting with the Lord.

3

He loved the world so much and showed
His love, giving his only begotten son,

Pledging only a desire for a sensible life.

I gave with my heart, getting precious things,
One by one,
Intervening slowly,
Extending a helping hand.

He gave faithful Job to the devil
Protecting and watching over him,
Seeing his constant thoughts,
And his faith that was true to the end.
The Lord called him a righteous man
And blessed him with abundance.

In faith,
Give away the dreadful mind,
And give away the body as it goes.

Thank
His hands that take

Your love that you share
Makes my heart tremble so,
Swollen with the joy of an unknown emotion.

4

As time passes, the Lord watches
Every corner of the mind.
With the blood and flesh of the Lord,
I can become a new person.

The soul starts yelling, sad and thirsty,
But then relaxes.

Led by the Holy Spirit,
It thinks and meditates.
I give my body and soul
To his wise will.

Always wait,
And think as much as you pray.
He says, "Understand my meaning,

And let us dream
Of an abundant world."

5

I feel urged to bury my past,
And take only hope.

Thrown into an open sea,
This is a lonely journey where none can find me.

Desperate to breathe,
I sense a strong feeling of being alive, a vital energy,
As I am led by you,
As I begin my life with you.

Murmuring from time to time
In a constant monologue,
The fools will be revealed
Rarely.
I conceal myself,
And make long time short.
The passionate love given by the cross
Helps me live.
I only wanted a new life.

☆ Ancestors were relieved
Take of yourself and give your body and mind to Him. Then you can
be a free and fluttering bird. Disregard the sound of struggle and the
collisions of futile lust if you want freedom of the soul. If you recharge
yourself with His words and love by thanking Him for today's life,
you can live the rest of your life thanking Him for providing daily
bread in spite of the stifling feelings of lonely reality. When you
lean on Him and do your best, with joy you can hear hope open.

Love

1

Confusion
That came from allurement:
Its mouth is open to swallow us.

Full of fear,
Full of doubts,
Your face fades in the darkness.
There will be no tomorrow for us.

Love,
It became a burning thirst,
Then got cold, as though chained.

Meaningless shadow of darkness,
My scar is getting worse
While wandering around this lightless world.

Finally,
I confess with tears and kneel down,
As Maria did to wait for mercy.

2

Uncovered shame is
Now touched by love.
You take away all distrusts
And dwell in the light.

Your mellow touch opens my heart.
Tears come out of my scar;
It is healed by your hand.

By your endless endurance,
My wickedness is gone.
Hardship is also done.
I drink the clear water of blessings.

Transcending all the sins,
You reign with compassion and say,
"You are my love; never be afraid."

3

The mist has now been cleared
And I see you coming.

Morning of forgiveness,
My soul is sparkling.

The greatest love remains in my fingers.
I touch and reach out to what I've got.
There, another soul is recovered.

In both of our minds
Flows the clean water of glory.
We cried together,
Buried hurts which were locked inside.

Purgatory isn't an issue,
But we're renewed by your name.
Whatever, whoever we were,
Your love compels us.

Oh, there's another soul I see,
With the same burning thirst as I had.

☆ Love
People are self centered. We complain about each other's selfish love
and get hurt, living in distrust. But why don't we open our hearts, love

ourselves first, and conciliate with others? We can forgive and hug all of the painful faults of this confusing world, embracing it with love. Because of love, we wish that tomorrow will be new and more beautiful. Because of our hopes, we dream of long lives. If you can tie and untie, you can build your own world, even if severe pain and suffering follow ...

Be a tall tree

1

Surging to the sky,
Moonlight shines or ripples
Through a colorful and fresh armful of leaves.
Youth's strength pours forward,
Stretched high in its composure,
And it overflows, like oil, with abundant, beauteous life.

2

A dull, shabby life
Floats, longing to fly in the sky,
Like a bird waiting for the time,
Just squatting and waiting for a chance.

Ask about our ancestors.
Let me pull out a bitter rock,
And see the tempest that is in front of destiny:
The wind keeps blowing,

Cultivating rough fields.
Keep picking out gravel,
Because if you turn your back, a hungry ghost appears,
Like invisible hope.

The devil of darkness appears,
Attacking on the street.
Each time, sprinkle the Lord's blood,
And confront him with strength.

Jehovah built a statue of faith,
Glorified you
Through his son's influence:
Cut off the rotten roots and start anew.

Each branch,
Soaked in sweet water,
Spurts new branches
With the strong energy of the earth.

3

Oh, a world of dreams opens,
Another fresh fruit of wonder.

Strong pillars are built on strong roots,
And will protect us from rain and wind.

Shining brightly,
This world will bear abundant fruit.

We are parts of one body,
And the mystery of life flows in you.

Look for the roots
And the blessing, as you become a tree of life.

Because of you,
Many people will eat and drink.

4

The ideal world is
A rising eagle that tears the darkness,

Is a tireless wing
That keeps rising up:

Be strong and bold.
Rise with large ambition.

Do not bother with stifling affairs.
Do not indulge in wealth and honor.

Enjoy the highest value
As you rise into a lofty world.

The roots of the soul grow deep,
And the love of the Lord will free you.

Days of new and creative plans will course through you,
And they will come.

☆ Be a tall tree
Our Lord, who built and shared the statue of faith, gave power to his only begotten son: to save and accompany all believers who changed to be like Him, to destroy evils on demand, to show us a new vision, and to keep creating and showing us the way to accomplish his dream.

Sailing

1

There's a bird
Flying hard against the current.

Sunshine glitters on the ocean;
It's a dream of freedom.

I lean back, heave out the anchor,
And shout out victory,
But only a silent echo comes back,
Then loses its direction and falls down.

My broken soul follows it,
Falls down to the end.

Against the dead pressure,
Sitting back on a transparent wall,
I flap my wings against the air in vain.

My body is rotten, without comfort,
And endless thirst's scratching my throat.

2

In front of my desires,
The anchor is settled.

My lonely voyage in the deep sea begins;
Strong winds and waves strike me all over.

I better take a deep breath
And lower my body.

Let me follow the hand of authority
Along the deep, dark sea.
And then it becomes a joyful surfing,
Sharing in the bread of life.

Golden sunshine gushes out,
Shining all over the sea.

"There is love,"
I'll say, scolding the rough waves.

The flow of freedom and the anchor of hope
Will raise me up and carry me on my way.

☆ Sailing

Don't be afraid of despair. The grace of God will remain for those who seek. Therefore, look for wisdom when you fall down. In the midst of hardness, try your best with thanksgiving. Enlarge your territory and look after others with composure. Then and there, your dreams will come true. Sincerely trust in this: I do not have fear because I lean on Him. It gives me the power of prayer, prayer that defeats the endless storms of life because He is with me. Keep proceeding each day while raising the anchor of hope. Wish for your victory. Let's lean on and trust love sincerely, which will help us until the end.

It is incredibly impressive. Everyday brings miraculous life. Breathing is dead silence until you meet perfect love. Dry wild flowers will die if not watered often. You will become the one who is vital, moving, and dreaming of the soul through His words.

2). Water turned into wine

1. Water turned into wine 1 2 3 4
2. Faith from conception 1 2 3
3. Holiness 1 2
4. The Cross 1
5. Dove of Holy Spirit

2). Water turned into wine

Water turned into wine

1

Ignorant and blinded,
In an unpredictable way,

Was the screaming voice of the soul.
If I carry light with an open mind,
I can see the twinkling star of myself,

Get a clear view,
And listen to what I wish to tell the Lord:
I rush to travel, taking

One step, and then another.
At the end of each corner there is a steep dirt road,
And I look for water in habitual ways.

The cracking earth has a coarse voice.
If I give my weary body

To your kisses,
Fresh and fragrant with violets,

Bountiful water gathers in my dry joints.
If I catch a stream that follows light,

Singing and jumping for joy,
It is like getting the whole world.

2

Like an unappreciated song,
A bird with no heart cannot fly.

A raging wind blows harder.
In the rugged valley, bones sleep on the road of Golgotha.

A cloud of doubt floats,
Bound by the world's custom.
It is fearful of being deserted and neglected,
And sees an intolerable sight in a crevice.

Even if shared love is shattered
Sad eyes still live in the comfort of a heart confined.

Perhaps
A vessel that never fills up
Might change a heart?

Even after straightening a collar
And cleaning a stifled heart,
Cold cannot be avoided.

In deep darkness,
His back is cold.

Even if I show my torn heart
And give my life,
The sorrow of not seeing you
Would dry my thirsty bones.

3

Anxious longing
Burns bone and bone marrow.
It can burn an entire body,
But the thorn bush will not burn.

The soul grows nervous and throws itself down harder,
But the burning flame never dies.

Hold your shoes
As you build an altar.

The Lord, Jehovah, descended Mountain Horeb,
And loved Israel's descendants through generations.
The sin was to distrust and turn
Toward a place of endless complaints and grudges.

He gave power through manna
And strength through words. Through forty years in the wild,
A cane did not burn even when held in flame,
for a sign of everlasting eternity.

He promised to his faithful descendants
A land of milk and honey.

4

He came with words
That filled up the container of eternity with spring water.
The Lord's love is like honeydew.

With His heart, hardened by law,
He gave order through His words;
The dry land was straightened.

He displayed the miracle
Of turning water into wine.

It was too young,
So it was aged for a long time
And filled with the water of life.

His love overflowed,
And songs of joy never ended.

As water flows,
Life also flows

All creatures breathe spring, summer, fall, and winter.

There is a flowing vitality in it, a bottomless taste.
Drunk with beautifully-colored wine,

They praised the Lord with love,
As water turned into wine.

☆ Water turned into wine
It is incredibly impressive. Every day brings miraculous life. Breathing
is like dead silence until you meet perfect love. Dry, wild flowers will die
if not watered often. You will become the one who is vital, moving and
dreaming of the soul through His words.

Faith from conception

1

Drunk with blessing,
A mother's unborn child is reborn in the Holy Spirit,
Forgiving sins of flesh:
A holy incarnation of love.

Protected by angels
In a deep valley of evil power,

Held as a blessing,
The gift of precious life
Given by the will of the Almighty.
It is a blessing and treasure from heaven.

When you stand with joy and envelope the power of darkness,
You can be approved for the blessing of children.

With yours,
Not mine,
Give me the dream of
Making history with faith.

2

Women!
Be like a dove.

Hold dreams of
Pure and holy incarnation.

A body builds a blessed castle
Through determined faith.

Bless yourself within,
To give fortunes to descendants of future generations.

Kneel obediently,
And walk within the will.

Wait patiently while you mature with love.
Do not lose the purity of your given life.

A chosen child during pregnancy
Will be used preciously, as a pillar.

He is the ruler of the world;
Who knew this before he was selected?

3

Beautiful women!
Be strong against seduction.

The mundane world
Is futile and vain.

Spare your efforts to stop decay,
Fueled by a fleeting desire.

Hold the new life
Of a creature.

Women are beautiful castles
In the Lord's world.

Like a pure dove,
Protect your body and soul.

The incarnation seeks the chaste
And blesses the chaste.

The fruit of the womb
Is the mother's prize.

☆ Faith from conception

He gave His only begotten son through Mary, who was pure, clean, and blessed. And so He continues to bless faithful women to carry out His will, even in times of corrupt morals and loose sex. He continues to protect our culture and society. Women! Be beautiful and strong and look far ahead, with eyes like a dove.

Holiness

1

A nature that
Cannot be formed without love,

Once it has lost its modesty,
Collapses in a moment.

Like dewdrops,
It must be collected daily
Or else it droops.

A mature love story is
Really hard to complete.

Trials and devotions
Will build a spirit of light, to please Him.

The shape of Jesus,
As a seed of words, blossoms into flesh

2

Ripe fruits of love
From thoughts and practices;

A living sacrifice
Of a bestowing life that comes from the heart;

An open mind
When praying and meditating, with good will;

The roots of holy faith,
Wholly adoring of the way Jesus took you up,

Like a pure white bunch of flowers,
Devoted, with different tints and talents;

A cup of grace and gratitude,
Where every step is offered as worship:

This is
Holiness.
It is the fragrance of a people
Who are seeking for everything that will accomplish the love of Christ.

☆ Holiness
It is for people more beautiful and fragrant than flowers. They trim pillars and improve the road to Heaven, like fair, white doves. This love our Lord gladly takes; then He shines it all over the world.

The Cross

1

Things that I've imagined are
Now locked in silent darkness:

A wheel of fortune
Tangled with stones that fly over my head, then stick,

A sinfulness deep inside of my soul.
I try hard to avoid these things,
But I'm lost, chained in a snare.

There is consistent temptation to be free from the restraints
All around me, all over me.
Satan's whisper still remains around my ears.

2

Bring the fire and
Light the lure on it.
Now love is frozen,
While despair is blazing.

There's a rough wave coming again.

Why?
Why?
I wonder and tremble.

At the moment, when fears come,
You come hold my hands
And make the wave calm.

I am begging underneath your feet, for mercy.

You just put the cross on my stiff body
And say, "It's yours, now follow me."

3

The love of taking away the
Privilege of children
I joined with joy, and made flames of fire.

I was like a small child:
Falling down and rising up;
Turned down, then begging again;
Crying out and reaching out my hands.

You came down like dew and
Forgave my sins.

Wickedness covers up Heaven's glory.
When praising, you should kneel down.
I'm joyfully reborn in spirit.

Your righteousness,
Words of wisdom:
My hope is to be humble,
Blessed by the crown of thorns.

Oh, love that shines upon us:
That's the love of the cross.

☆ Cross
It is the endless war against oneself. We would never be able to win without faith; it cannot be shared without love. When we follow the Lord, carrying the cross, we can control light and darkness. It is a beautiful crown in life that we can achieve by conquering temptations.

Dove of Holy Spirit

Between heaven and earth,
Under the free wind
There flies a dove of Holy Spirit.

It is the purest thing,
A love of white light,
Spreading peace to the world.

A life is like a visitor;
It shortly comes and goes,
But you seed and harvest,
Give and take away.
It's a combination of thunder and lightning,
Renewing every single life.

Each of the changing seasons,
Even one of the grass blades on a hill:
Everything is in His hands.

Then why follow the world, and seek vanity?
Why be slaves of it?

Instead, be in the love of the Holy Spirit,
Flying towards the ideals
Every day, new and fresh as a dove.

☆ Dove of Holy Spirit
Everyone has purpose in his life. It's either big or small, high or low.
Anyhow, it exists like a tree. According to what we pursue, our appearance
changes. Therefore, why don't we bloom with smile? Remember: our
purpose in life is to praise our creator. That's the life of meaningfulness
and happiness, achievable with the help of the Holy Spirit.

Love with the almighty; if I can use a small gesture to become starlight,
I will keep burning my sinful body and soul.

3). Truly, truly

1. Truly, truly 1 2 3 4 5
2. Mother 1 2 3 4
3. Wilderness 1 2
4. In front of the Lord 1 2
5. New Jerusalem

3). Truly Truly

1. Truly Truly 1 2 3 4 5

1

Truly, the
Love of the cross was given free of charge.

He created a universe

From himself, by giving his son,
Who redeemed our sins.

He is abundant in this world,
Giving power to the sky,

And holding life, each single life,
As the soul's food, as that which revives life.

He holds it righteously,
And freely gives it manna to eat.

Rather than flesh,
The promise of salvation makes up the life of the Lord.

2

This precious gift was given for free,
And transformed into ability.
He bled your blood for such a paltry sum,
While crying out with the voice of power!

Telling every sin of Judas,
Like solving a sacred mystery.

He kept working and renewing life,
While crying out with the Holy Spirit's despair.

They were confined by fear,
And buried the joy of freedom in reality,
Confusing flesh and soul,
Holding on to the blessings of a thieving world,
Adding new faith to old faith,
Panting.

Water dried up, and
Deep crevices kept cracking wider, with urgency.

Heave well. If you cannot hold the world,
Pressed by sin,
Perhaps you cannot because you are not saved?

Struggling to achieve a great vision,
You must cross forests, that are like skyscrapers,
That try to devour you.

Seek water with a hungry stomach
When you are wandering in the woods.

Why go higher?
Why dignify life's value
When comparing it to the mundane world?

Climb a high mountain,
Seeking the water of life, in this urgent time!

3

Wake the sleeping soul.
This is the true love, that of awakening from the mundane.
Just like the love of the cross, it is getting stronger,
Revealing the sin and carnal desires of the flesh.

As a messenger of light,
He built a temple of Jerusalem in his heart,

Holding and propping it up.
Awakened by the destruction of the evil power of the devil,
He came to serve,
And gave peace and joy.

Come to the lowest place.
Your true love redeems our sins.
Give the true freedom of salvation,
And liberate us from sin.

His vision is of
Peace for mankind, through love.

Through faith
His kingdom follows the mind's light, and it
Will soon be built

4

His righteousness was revealed,
As though by light.
In love he would not give up even the life
That was planned and executed.

A thousand years seem the same as one day
In your heart that never changes.

Even if nearsighted eyes
Were blocked,
Betrayed countless times,
And became sinful,

He would endure longer and forgive,
With a glass full to the brim with sincere blessings.

When the body is worn out
By the soul, the love of salvation
Lets us kneel and be reborn.

A life rots, turns into wheat berry.
Our brothers and sisters
Are bound, without words and blessings.

Waves of gospel reach the ends of the earth.
The cross of the Lord is the joy of all mankind.

5

You did not know that love is bound to happen
While you were wandering, without a destination.
Suddenly, one day,
He saw you,

Like a newborn child,
White and clean.

He shone glorious light to the faithful tribes of Israel,
Lit the darkness for the disciples of the Lamb of God.
The great love of the Lord
Makes life like pure gold.

Light flows inside of the heart
While the river of life overflows.

Newly reborn companions
Are in the holy temple,
Where they built the kingdom of the Lord.

They will enjoy true freedom,
And peace will prevail on earth.

☆ Truly, Truly

Overflowing abundance is the joy of seeing Him, because the breath of life can be heard inside the heart, and a life that praises glory will flow and become a river. Truly, truly, you become a power to help the humble and shining lives of those who practice the love of God. Praises to the Lord upon his plans, for the good news will reach to the ends of the earth, and the world will be tied together with peace and love. Nevertheless, among overflowing blessings, there remains spiritual hunger and poverty. Therein lies disassociation, confusion in mind, poorness, and an illness that is all over the earth.

We're dying under the ruins of war. But I still pray that the vision of Christ is proclaimed, and that He reigns, through His chosen people, so that the victory of Christ is accomplished with love and prayers.

Mother

1

When love grows,
The world of suffering can be withstood.

The mother's life flows,
And Buddha's mercy for the child is wholehearted.

How can you say that
The heart is futile?

It is the place where you stayed for a short time,
In a mother who thought honestly
And only walked the straight path,
She lived her entire life on that path,
With sincerity and devotion.

2

The mother's heart aches
When she cannot give enough.

Concerned for a long time,
She turns her back and sheds tears.

Solace from the Holy Spirit
Took over her life.

You walked through, and
Comforted her heart.

Now look up
And see the sky.

Put down life's worries,
And hold the light of eternity.

3

The mother took only the straight road, stubborn.
She only wanted to live honestly.

Seeing the outcome of the earth,
She did not hear it

Because it was too early.
Its insufficiency was hidden.

There is nothing to show
In resignation that parades as despair.

You cannot relieve the soul at will;
My spirit is restless.

If not parents, brothers, or sisters,
Who will take that road?

With an impatient heart,
You end up kneeling and begging with tears

The voice of God said
That you were redeemed a long time ago.

4

He who proclaimed the gospel to the ends
Of the earth has a plan.

Look forward to the
Proven power of the new kingdom.
The last will become the first.

Children who know God's will:
Do not judge and punish the superficial.
They are used
In a different way.

He who respects others, and obeys humbly
Will be admired with gratitude.

Through reborn children,
His love is revealed and expanded.
Build a history of redemption,
For He is the Savior and King of the universe.

☆ Mother

If you treat others like the devil because of your incorrect views of religious belief, it can block your road to the Lord. Do not forget that you can become an enemy and play the devil's role. Even if your mouth calls to the Lord, if you do not take the straight path in your life and do not understand its meaning, it is the same as committing a crime. Why? Because you will still be a prisoner behind the door of darkness. The one who has love does not punish, but instead keeps growing and is devoted.

Wilderness

1

Through dense skyscrapers,
Cold light falls.

You can hear the heavy breath of
Wandering angels
With hungry love.

Turning their backs,
Many people move quickly,
And even pass those in front of them.
With dark eyes, they cannot see each other.

Fully on earth,
Hold every richness and
Lonely despair, while you walk in shackles.

Everyone's consciousness is getting clearer,
And they yell up. to the splendor,

But the sound only dissipates
Into a faint echo.

2

The cane of Moses
Is not noticed

Amid too many blessings
And great hunger.

Dream of living,
And seeking endlessly,
Laying down, stroking your stomach.

The world is full of
God's wisdom.

Untruth runs rampant,
And bleakly reveals bone.

Those who have good eyes
In the face of consciousness
Will fill with the pure water of life.

They hold the glory of the cross,
Like the voice of someone crying in the wilderness
For peace and love!

☆ Wilderness

If you climb a mountain with your will, you will get stronger. If you climb a mountain with God's blessing, your spirit's eye becomes clearer and can see the way. When the spirit's eye opens, you live an insightful life, but if you are confined, you run ceaselessly, trying to fill your hungry stomach. If your strong will stands straight before God, you can keep everything you want, past the valley of the desert ...

In front of the Lord

1

People who will enter the New Jerusalem will gather here
And become free by cutting off the chains of sin.
Born again with words, they open the gates
of Heaven with praise and pray,
"Let us achieve our dream of seeking the Holy Spirit."

Sit here to earn God's love.
Get holy; get stronger.
When we defeat the devil and worship God,
Our dreams open and Jerusalem's gates open.

Remember the Savior's voice as it tells us to cry out.
If the Lord answers, we can ask for His love.
It is a place where we achieve our requests and continue to shine by
Looking wisely to the road that the Savior walked,

Earning love by the redemption of the cross,
Nailing up our sins, and living as His children.
Let us witness the road Christ walked.
The promise of redemption brightens because He loves the world.

2

In a place where priest and believer are united as one,
Kneel and learn spirituality.
In a place where you stand straight as the words of truth,
Awaken to the love that God shares.

Even if problems arise during the course of life,
We will be joyful and free on the road, accompanying the Lord.
Even if rugged mountains block the road,
We will enter Jerusalem and unload our sin.

Give appreciation, with the service of your united body and soul.
Though you may be faithful, you cannot reap if
you are lazy and have nothing to give.
The pious spirit that is closed should repent and be forgiven.

When righteousness is revealed by God's calling,
The kingdom of light will be built without punishment.
He is the love and savior of mankind;
Praise and worship Him.

☆ In front of the Lord
The invisible nourishment of prayer and filial piety can help you even if you are rooted in the wrong place—you will grow strong like a rock, and prosper. You will solve the world's problems without living a difficult life. You can accomplish this through your faith, if you recover and revive your relationship with God and command spiritual authority.

New Jerusalem

Our souls
Are the starry lights of the Lord.
While burning with lightning,
He rules with joy and love,
Taking glory, giving nobility during suffering,
And consoling your tears with sympathy.
God is alive.
Praise and glorify Him.

Be with us,
Noble love of God.
Do you know that the Lord's making turned us into lights?
His plan will be achieved before us.
Our Lord
Is delighted and blesses us,
Freeing us from sin.
Let us sing to Him and praise Him.

Shine, with your heart polished.
Renew your spirit.
God holds His pure love.
Where are the people who will take joy in burning?
The New Jerusalem is dawning,
As the promise of redemption is delivered.
Praise and glorify
Our Lord.

☆ New Jerusalem
I find love with the Almighty; if I can use a small gesture to become
starlight, I will keep burning, purging my sinful body and soul.

We all have hard times that we want to run away from. But if we don't solve it, somebody else should do. Have humble and mature personality to bare the situation. Walk with Jesus who wants to carry your burden. You'll be full of joyfulness.

4). Overcoat

1. Overcoat 1 2 3 4
2. Yoke
3. Test 1 2
4. Reconciliation
5. Blessing

Overcoat

Overcoat

1

Buried by the shadow of delusion,
His love came on winding roads.

Try to touch the invisible light,
As you believe what is uncovered, as love.
He dresses me as the season changes, and an overcoat emerges.
I dream a seven color, rainbow dream.

He thought love was this size.
He built a house inside of thought.

Accumulating the smell of malt,
His mind keeps wandering

Drinking wine,
He toasts for a change:
Give my body to Thy will,
As I look around in the pitch black.

Do not desert me.
Hold me with a soft kiss.

He knew what was already needed,
In wise consideration
That only can be seen
While holding a gentile's outer garments,
And begging for love.
His gloomy mood was not known.

2

It seems like creatures are destined
To be buried in sin, falling in the wind.

But because he loves us
And treats us with sincerity,

He cleans our blood,
And lets it flow into a new life.

Come here,
And wait to be seen as light.

3

If he hides for a while,
Lost, seated,
Prostrate—you can see it is not enough,
And you must serve and obey.

With his great love,
He renews and soothes us.

Pouring oil
And engaging evermore
In a gift of trust,
He removes his overcoat.

Righteous, he calls to
The trusting heart and its following.

Let us see love revealed,
And our goal met as we
Visit the dark valley of the woods.
And let us confess into His hand, the one that holds ours
In front of the soul that blooms like flowers.
For you a dream is growing

I want to give my life to God, made of
Only my love and faith.

4

Shaking in misery,
Some question love.

Life is less important than the dust
That illuminates light.

Impure, exposed rock
Is shattered to pieces.

Pure crystal
Overflows with words of love,

A tool used to achieve his will
And prepare an overcoat of resurrection.

☆ Overcoat
Ease come, easy go. Even if you take the whole world, if you do not get
a new life, it will still rot as a trifle rots. You cannot see the beauty of
resurrection, made of His love. Like a thick tree that grows unnoticeably
and forms annual rings, our insides should grow layer upon layer to the
point that we can show enduring strength against fierce winds. Water,
nourishment, and love take all. Only faith to Him promises abundance
of the soul, because He prepares our overcoat.

Yoke

Hug the pain;
Close the eyes.

The roaring soul settles down;
A mellow serenade falls down.

One way,
One light-filled way:
It's a promise of salvation that
Motivates me to walk again,
When stuck in the narrow alley.

As well as you say,
"The yoke is mine,"
Oh, your love gushes out and redeems.

It's your calling in the midst of difficulties.
I sing your true love with freed heart.
I'll walk along the way of light.

☆ Yoke

We all have hard times that we want to run away from. But if we don't solve them, somebody else should. Have a humble and mature personality, to bear the situation. Walk with Jesus, who wants to carry your burden. You'll be full of joyfulness.

Test

1

Despite deep affection,
You put him in a muddy swamp.

He was surrounded by seven devils,
Going up and down the Golgotha hill.

The deepest shame comes out
Of all earthly sins.

During the test, which you allow,
He screams from the pain of breaking bones.

Is it all for me to show your will,
That you let Him suffer?

2

The tired soul is drawn into a hollow;
Evils rush at me and tear me apart.

But the love of much caring
Is in my lord's righteousness.

His shedding of blood for every single life is
Soaked in my body, warm and bright.

His authority drives away devils
By revealing Satan's weakness to us.

Our Lord, who came by hatching from love into a new life,
By Heaven's authority, he is called the Son of God.

☆ Test

As God reveals his will through his people, Satan also slyly comes to people's mind and allures, leading them to collapse. We are fragile in that it is easy to lose our minds; therefore, consistent prayer seeking wisdom is important. At the time that we're in a test from God, we should defy devils in the name of Christ, to conquer them. Always be aware of whether I'm at Satan's side. Stay up in the way of God the Father.

Reconciliation

A shock of awakening shows hurt
And scratch marks. Are they the
Inevitable storms of life?

Raging waves can be traced,
As the noisy foam of rage
Dies down
Into the silence of the deep sea.

You must struggle endlessly,
In a consolation match that cedes no winner.
Even if time changes things,
A hurt, stained, and touched wound
Would be the result of not forgiving ourselves.

Held
Under his wing,
You only need to stay quiet.

A green spring arrived before, cleaning the old stain.
I cried as it was soaked, slowly.

Is there any hope,
Or do you want to cry, overwhelmed with shame?
We,
With silent, clear eyes,
Know that only love breaks the heart.

☆ Reconciliation
You seek the Lord's love in various forms, large and small, and in pain.
Husbands, children, parents, and brothers put up with each other
sometimes, and reveal vice and foolish behavior at other times. They
shed shameful tears behind each others' backs. You should beg for his
mercy and strength without giving up. A prayer is awakened first. The

Lord will show you a righteous road and solutions to problems when you achieve His will. If you believe in His love, even big problems can be treated maturely.

Blessing

Graceful love
Redeems her faith as she digs into the fountain of wisdom.

Deeper and
Wider,
The blessing of new life opens:
It will be honored with a devoted and humble mind

When frightened
By fear and suffering,
Feel the will of praise and hope,
And the great love of God.

Oh! Her faith resides in wisdom,
And even the suffering of the cross is enough.

Fortunate,
Beautiful,
Blessed on the rock,
She encounters ancient waiting.

With faith and hope
God became the light of love. He consoles
With song and joy,
Sacrifice and comfort.

Even though you dig and
Dig, thoughtful love
Never dries up. It will last forever.

Give the blessings of family
To God, who came back to life.

☆ Blessing

God sees, listens, and knows. He wants to have a close relationship with each one of us; to accompany and console us; to take care of inevitable affairs; to forgives us and encourage us, even in our deficiencies; to accept us as we are; to give us the victory of the cross by loving us; and He wants us to enjoy a life of rest.

It is bothersome that I used words like philosophy. I fight
to keep my position. Fighting with an idea shows only self-
absorption. I want to pour words of love, hope, and praise. I want
to express this. Philosophy without God falls into darkness.
It cannot see the eternity of God and the world of love.
Even if you could see bright hope, it would not last.

5). The narrow road

The narrow road 1-18

The narrow road

The narrow road

1

In the wind's voice is
Wind's temptation,
Wind's insanity
And its folly.

Do not ask why I take this road
That is full of wisdom,
And speak frankly.

An encounter with nature is like a festival,
Where life's scents wraps your body,
Carried by rhythms of the wind,
And flies to dancing lunatics who dream of deadly spirits.

2

Restless is
Wind's fleeting sound through bamboo fields.

Split bamboo breaks easily, they say,
Bounces away,
Inconsiderate.
Are you the only one
Whose superiority is rewarded?
Be a decent man,

A weary mother pleads,
Do not follow customs anymore.

3

A gust of wind shrieks,
While a sinner suffers aches,
Alone.

Listen to faint sounds.
Make a complete confession,
As if suffering comes from sin.
From life's ties, love flows.
Forget to solve life's problems.
Look to be blessed,
To follow the law;
Try to live a pious and ornate life.

4

He dreams of living life like a dance:
Carried away by the wind's temptation,
Tumbling over the earth,
Filthy and dirty.
Muddy water splashes.
Does he have any principles?
Should he be committed?

But, here and there,
He sees it,
The gem he must dig for during his struggling life.
It shines there,
Where wild rumors run rampant,
Where stones pour out gloom and darkness.

5

He declared, "I cannot live like a pendulum,
Stirring time
As if night is day,
As if morning is night,

Deceiving and deceived, unknowingly
Working for work's sake."
He set his mind desperately on plans with no fruit,
Just to live.

They regard him as talented, though
He seems madly obsessed with work.

6

His madness
Was lonely. He was sad, at the bottom of his fall,
Thinking about things over and over.

He had to stand on his feet, and find the
Motivation to alleviate the suffering
That he caused.
He threw himself onto a rock,
Expanded his world as a man with a new mission:
Instead of using bloody endeavors
To make a living,
He stood and blocked scornful,
Irresponsible words.
An invisible bud grew deep inside,
Understood by no one.

Risking his life,
He spent half of it in pursuit,
And liberated me
From all risks, but also from all comforts.

In my heart, I expected him.
I wished for a strong tow.

7

Only the beginning exists:
Endless wilderness, and a

Resolute spirit, fearless
Like a roaring lion. he opens his mouth and
Looks up at the sky,
Arrested by the devil in life's wilderness.
He must make many journeys,

Must find out what hell is,
What the world is,
Like a messenger of the Lord.

He will work hard.
Life is as empty as a bubble.

8

Stone showers down, like
Broken family affairs. There are personal attacks in the paper,
As if the writers are perfect.
As they sling mud and harass him,
He smiles silently.
He does not stop them or defy them,
Or blow them away with one breathe from behind.

His passion stands firm, for work and love.
Like a pilgrim of penance,
He went there, even though he found nothing.
He had to go, he had to go,
And he tried even harder.

9

Even though everyone around him tired of his passion and love,
Even though they could not do the same,
Even though they caused suffering,
His passion and love
Radiated constantly.

Why?

For what?

Many sinners surrounded him.
Everyone: parents, siblings, children.
They knelt and reflected deeply,
Begged for mercy,
And dedicated their love to him, as they did to the Lord.

Then they all fell,
Into larger love and blessing.

10

The war caused this.
Torn, slashed, and stained eyes,
Marked with sorrow and despair.
Commanding like a warrior, he traversed the minefield
With something silent that sparkled
Deep inside of him.
No one understands the journey of life.

11

It is beautiful because of the fierce struggle.
Walk the crazy road and become a sinner.
But look at the sacred road, and see:
The confession scene is
Beautiful as a dove.

Inside of eyes washed clear with the muddy water of life,
You will find loneliness and pity, endlessly repeating over time.
The meaning of life is loneliness.

The same thing begins again,
Intrinsic to its nature:
Patience always suffers.

12

He met madness,
Fought temptation,
Stormed in his penance,
And betrayed love
While hot with the diligence
Of a larger love and passion.
He thrust his head onto rocks repeatedly,
While sharing joys and sorrows.

Catch every hallucination
And keep it as if it were mine.
Disturb everything violently,
And cause embarrassment while going wild.

13

The wind takes away
Many things in its gusts.
Even rotten roots are torn up and hurled.

Life with its thorns is lit afire
And blazes uncontrollably.

14

Without principle and courage,
Continue forward:
Publicly, and privately.

Forgive over seventy times.
Obtain love and trust.
He was resolved to get something
In the dark corners of the world,
Even by disgracing himself.
He longed to look for, to see the
Lord's creation

His world was in the middle of the road,
A world he could achieve by sacrificing himself.
Still, there was something only the Lord knew,
And he was still trapped inside of it.

15

In the name of love,
Starts fights, wars in which to kill and be killed.
Falling wounded in the lonely night sky,

Bound by determination and the desire for comfort
He forgave himself, reaching an inner reconciliation.
Because of raging winds against the cliffs,
I saw the open road of a dream and made a pledge in front of him.

Enthusiasm and love grew deeper,
Leading the world with explosive energy.
I am burning with longing for it.

Oil stood in a corner of his path.

Long before,
A long time ago,
So many stars burned with faith,
And shed light along the road.

Love, a large star,
Sends dreams to the soul,
And brightly illuminates things .

16

Finally, in the dark
I could smell a fragrance, my
True image through the course of a kaleidoscopic life.
I was also part of nature.

In the bosom of a supreme ruler,
I returned to a life of nature,
Singing love and living in a wave's torrent.
I became a bird,
And could find the color and love
Of the blood that runs through the soul

17

Wind, wind, wind:
He will face one that arrives on the wind.
Husbands and wives, do not despair.
There is so much to throw away.
After you put down the heavy load,
You will realize the Lord is there.
Instead of the pain of looking for a
Shield from life's path of agony,
Which will stop the shivering of the wind,
We stood together in hellfire.
The shrub's love will kindle and burn a bush of thorns
To ashes, and there will be a taste: the flame's meaning.

You will surely understand that
The old becomes the new,
Becomes a new sky and earth, and
Takes the position of beautiful nature.

18

There is a tree,
An apple tree of lost paradise.
There is a universe, a world where
Water rolls,
And there is no fear of the freedom needed to flow.
It can be shared with everyone.
Soul's pleasure exists
Without the seven-color rainbow that is rising,
Without the bright light of gems.

Throw it away, throw it all away
Burn it away, burn it all away

The kingdom's righteousness is made of
Transparent love.
Eat and drink with Him, and
Live in the green grass of a lost paradise.

Dance with the Lord,
And you will enjoy creation and love.

☆ The narrow road
It is bothersome that I used words like philosophy. I fight to keep my
position, but fighting with an idea shows only self-absorption. I want to
pour words of love, hope, and praise. I want to express this. Philosophy
without God falls into darkness. It cannot see the eternity of God and
the world of love. Even if it can see bright hope, it will not last.

So many people dream of the beautiful life of giving, longing to share
with an open heart. But we hate, and turn back because of small
misunderstandings, wounds, and betrayals. One-sided love that does
not consider others cannot last long. It seems like giving, but can
become greedy. In your family or work place, everyone's life is like your
precious neighbor. Not only through volunteer work, but also through
self-review, will you be able to see if you are right. Also, service to society
and devotion will help achieve His love and will be changed by His light.
You can dream of true love longer as the waves of light get wider.

Suffering with faith becomes the origin of strength,
opening your eyes with hope helps you seek dreams,
and sharing time with love achieves peace.

6). Thorn Bush Love

1. Thorn Bush Love 1 2 3 4 5 6
2. New Sky and New Earth 1 2 3
3. Resurrection
4. Recognition of the Soul

Thorn Bush Love

Thorn Bush Love

1

Keep loving Him,
Even if you are thrown into the fire.

It is eternal life

That you meet in flames of fire.
It is deepening love.

2

I saw His plans
And His glory
Rolling in the dirt,
Like a sharp stone about to be kicked.
As it is with the most immoral,
Estranged, profound love:
Only with obedience and
Complete emptiness can you
Reach His goal.
On the unyielding road of destiny,
In complete darkness,
The thorn bush's love burns with words.

3

Tangled, shaggy,
Thorny bush of the world,
Twisted by the devil
And hoping for a high mountain:

It burns with words.

The promise of eternal life is in fire, which is
The rescue of light.

4

From time immemorial breathes
Deeply-rooted love.

The pained cry of a thing bound to the earth
Shatters the heart.

It wails while taking root in the earth,
Thirsty for the earth.
A mother who cannot abandon anything
Calls for help while holding a child.

Open words.
While sky and earth unite,
Creatures are raised in love and sympathy:
Their lives on earth are united as one,
And so it goes, round and round.

5

With the love of a cross
He broke a blocked wall.
Sky and earth:
Make them one.

6

As it deepens,
The thorny bush has flesh that burns with love.

Like a thorn bird, it is
Thick with yearning and hungry with desire.

Burned,

Everything is burned.
If I saw you appear suddenly in flames,

The glowing love inside of me would
Turn its light toward Him.

After erasing all the sinful
Thorns of flesh,

We can live forever
In His kingdom full of souls.

☆ Thorn bush love
This road we follow
Is burning in a sea of flames,
Because words are aflame in the shrub.

Sometimes our will creates the Tower of Babel.
A life of obedience
Hears the smooth voice of love, even in a deep valley
Understanding this life is a blessing

New Sky and New Earth

1

The sky hears
Earth's scream.

Earth accepts the sky's
Collapsing roar.

Those who dream of a
New sky and a new earth

Are those who listen to
Suffering and love, which coexist.

2

For those who take off their shoes,
There is a holy place
Where the glorious sky fulfills the earth.
You will see the burning thorn bush's love,
And a new sky and earth will open.

3

Everything comes from the Lord:
Abundant land, where there are only blessings and appreciation.
And everything goes to the Lord.

With love,
Full of the fruits of joy, and
With faith,
You can see what is holy and divine
In the scripture of the mind.

☆ New Sky and New Earth

Life passes, futile and vain. If we see that tomorrow will be renewed by God, we can be creatures that belong there. We trust His acts, expect His continued love, and live and dream joyously. You and your children will accomplish the dream of the almighty, will be awakened continuously, will pray to be used by Him, and will open your hearts.

Resurrection

I'm not going to doubt.
I'm not going to ask,
Because it is the way to follow you.

Though it is not easy at all,
As with fatal disease, I am
Isolated from the world.
Or as with loss of sight, I am
Not able to see the light of a high mountain.

Still, I can feel your breath.
I can touch your robe.

Then I will go to your sea,
Where I'll never be thirsty, but will be filled
With Heaven's glory and love.

☆ Resurrection

Doing anything you can, while doing your best, means that you are aware of reality. The more reality there is in my dreams and in my longing to create my kind of world, the more my soul becomes beautiful. It is an endless war I fight with myself. Now I have to dig, dig silently like a mole.

Recognition of the Soul

My groom,
My master!
Descended with glorious,
Countless angels. They circle around you
On your leaf of a throne.
You are full of whispering stars.

Your kingdom is governed gracefully.
Your golden crown glitters,
A mark of righteousness that shines on the world.

Your deep and strong eyes
Are aflame with love and passion, big enough
to encompass the universe.
Because of the pouring oil's glory,
Flowering purity pulls back the curtain of sin,
Naming all creatures,
Flying down like a dove,
And baptizing everyone with the Holy Spirit.

With love,
The Lord flew on,
Rippling life with His blessings and sympathy.
While the water of life flew over each valley,
Dry bones danced.
Spirits were soaked with aged red wine.
Brides in white prepared oils.

They call to the golden field,
And skip about while holding your hand.

Sweet and pleasant
Is the aroma of lips.
Milk and honey overflow, through the open door
That invites us into a warehouse full of God's food.

King of such a kingdom, and master,
My groom!

A Blind Bird cannot see the Scarecrow.
Only the master's voice and the love of golden fields
can accompany this eating and drinking ...

☆ Recognition of the Soul
Suffering in faith becomes the origin of strength, opening your eyes
with hope. It helps you seek your dreams, and sharing time in love helps
you achieve peace.

If you love more, it is pure and beautiful. The eyes of the soul become clearer as you sublimate things inside of you. He gave us our lives by giving His only begotten son. Move closer to the creator and wish to dream fully of peace and love by the true light of your hear. When you love with all your heart, abundance, that has been held, grows bigger.

7). **Poppy**

1. Poppy
2. Sea
3. Beautiful Temptation
4. To love is

Poppy

Poppy

Like rubbed,
Blooming, dark red love

At an unsafe and prohibited water level,
An artificial flower is thrown.

Dried up in the face of reason,
When the bottom is turned up,
The heartbreake spews poison.

Stronger than light
That holds the shadow of death
Is the burning flame of a profound abyss.

Sip
By sip,
A cool black heat comes.

Shrinking if it overflows,
Deepening when your breath is held,
It never changes, always fascinates.

It must be drunk for you to live,
Just break the shell and

Follow the reverberation of the soul.
Blooming, dark red longing is

Quickly smeared.
It can be medicine or disease,
This mysterious drug.

☆ Poppy

Buds of sin grow very quickly in the heart. If you leave them alone, they sicken your body and tie it up, so that love stops. If you beg for righteousness from God and mediate on a new life, the buds of sin will be cut away, and you will see your face fill with joy. He wants everyone to feel His love and enjoy its abundance with others.

Sea

Even deep sorrow is muddied
When it is left floating on water.
These deposits settle: pain, desire,
Heartbreak, persistence, and yearning

Stay in your breath to become the
Happiness of a sensible life.

Even a body covered in wild insanity
Can move on with the passing breeze,
Because you can catch love,
And call it a deep sea.

Blue and cold, it is a desire
You are unable to lift.
It calls for all eternity.

☆ Sea

Thinking and doubting are the stones in life that endure storms, but
this is necessary in the process of stones becoming crystals. You must be
alive. You must be awakened. You must learn to listen to the sound of
the soul. Do not say that you are not full, because God loves us all. If you
understand the reality of God, you want His other world as well. If you
do not know this reality, you struggle ceaselessly to know it.

Beautiful Temptation

Nature whispers.
All of nature gestures to Him.
Give love to everyone;
You cannot fathom His profound mind.

If you see Him once,
You will fall in love
With the expression of His elegant figure.
He visited me and
Said that He loves me.

A worthless life
Will win, with faith.

Listen and follow His voice.
Empty your eyes and mind.
We shared hot blood:

As you are the only one in me,
I will live in Him.

☆ Beautiful Temptation
Sound. Sound. Even if it is a miserable and hurtful sound, my heart will
sing in earnest. What am I now? Oinking like a pig, confined in a pen
and waiting for the Savior to throw me a line. Indeed, where is God's
will? Do we pray and wait? Follow clues to find a tasty cake? My plan
is to wait earnestly, to seek the hidden treasure in the ashes, that tasty
cake. I was changed in this way.

To love is

To love is

To let go, while stepping into the light
That sends dreams into the soul.

To love is
To walk, leaving footprints
That make a bridge to the heart.

To love is
Not to ask for the road of return.
Pulled by soul's power,
We understand each other through the light in which we walk.

And love is
Like a quick-running water
That leads us to each other,
Joining us in a deeper place.

You cannot catch the form: it is
Without size, body, or reason.

☆ To love is
If you seek love more, this is pure and beautiful. The eyes of the soul
become clearer as you sublimate things, draw them inside yourself. He
gave us our lives by giving His only begotten son. Move closer to the
creator, and wish for dreams that are full of peace and love, lit by the true
light of your heart … When you love with all your heart, the abundance
that you hold grows bigger.

"Words attached Article"

No one wants to lose his voice as he lives his life. Also, if you ask anyone, you will find that each person's life is full of stories. You will realize that these stories could fill more than one volume of fiction. If you look at the world, it is full of a countless number of individuals. At a glance, they all look similar, but through close observation, you see they all look different. In other words, many people will go through similar trials, but if you consider the difficulties posed by these trials, they are each different, and the solutions to them are different for each individual.

In the hierarchy of society, one's life does not seem special. We experience sadness and happiness in individual manners, and through these experiences we grow differently. Likewise, happiness is experienced differently and individually, and unless this is recognized by both parties, it will be impossible to develop a relationship that is true. This lack of understanding will lead to estrangement. Without respect for one another's internal feelings, it is impossible to have a real relationship and meeting of minds. In this manner, the writer and readers' meeting as individuals should come from a place of respect.

When you first read these poems, your first impression is a personal testament of an encounter with the Lord. We witness the courage of the writer. Instead of avoiding suffering, we see the speaker deciding to walk the road of suffering instead. This is a very unique method of living, because, it is one that does not try to avoid suffering, but chooses instead to walk across the hard ground and awaken the spirit of the Lord within. He does not make a goal for us to walk toward or seek to hold onto a stronghold, but rather He waits to meet us, though we cannot see Him.

At this point, we can compare religion with lack of religion, God with the absence of God, as different human beings have different views. By living through many contradictions and pains, you try to listen to your own mind honestly. After much trial, you can really hear the honest voice of your inner soul. At this point, there are no regulations. There are no finite guidelines. In this language of passionate moment, there is freedom from all known guidelines.

I learned from this poem that I am not trying to go back to prior guidelines, but instead I am trying to see current viewpoints. In so doing, I come to realize what it is that I really want. This poem shows me a path. It clearly visualizes the greatness of the current situation, even though the world is not complete. Instead of a mindset of emptiness, it offers a way to rise out of suffering and sadness. This brings you to a meeting with the Lord, and this takes courage. In human relationships, strife comes when you don't take into account differences.

This poem also comes from many minor viewpoints that I personally hold and that I try to hold onto subconsciously. I am trying to emulate a child's mind by putting down my own guidelines and meeting the Lord with innocence. I do this by letting go, so that I can go where I must go and have the freedom to go there. In this freedom, there is no goal setting or holding on, just an endless effort to grow.

This is really what is most beautiful in the state of human beings.

Sungkyung Yun
Lecturer, Myeongji University
Institute of Continuing Education

When we just wait and wait, wander

When we just wait and wait, wander,
Our soul is in dark, fighting with inner lust.
Let us pray once more.
As there are four different seasons,
Our spiritual relationship has seasons too.

We try to do something with
Sadness, sorrow, complication, and delusion.
We follow our own will, only to find that
We're lost, directionless, and nothing's changed.

But how lucky that we have our Father.
We can surrender to the Almighty!

With a deep breath, a new life is opening.
Trusting the Lord helps the heart.
With the grace of faith, hope, and love,
The times of endurance and hardship can become a poem.
This poem has an aesthetic of sorrow.

When we're nourished by precious life,
And the love of Christ, which is wisdom,
Our wickedness and weakness are
Covered over and changed into the joy of truth.

Now we can conquer any mountain, with firmly founded faith.
It's free sailing in all the matters that weigh upon us.
Positive and bright days are waiting, and
Nothing can keep us down.

Our short-term thoughts and passions,
All dissatisfaction and complaints,
They're replaced by Life in Christ,
Which means our souls dwell in him and
His words become our body.

Though life is not that easy,
If we walk with Jesus,
The glory of Christ is with us.
We see our ills and throw them away.
We're renewed by the light of Love.
Finally, we'll enjoy the most beautiful and precious
Eternal life, forever and ever.

"And this gospel of the kingdom will be preached in the whole world as a testimony to all nations, and then the end will come." Matthew 24:14

About the Author: Miree Ban

Born in 1962 in Young-Kwang, Jollanamdo, Korea, she had a vision and a dream and decided to come to the United States in 1990. She expected  changes in this new world, and made her life in New York. She was educated at the Christine Balmy International School in the fields of international skin peeling and permanent makeup professional study. After obtaining her license, she won an award at the International Beauty Competition in New York. She is an instructor of healthcare business training at the Flushing Community Development Center in New York and is currently operating in the Korean makeup and skincare business at the same time that she does her work with spiritual poetry.

www.ingramcontent.com/pod-product-compliance
Lightning Source LLC
Chambersburg PA
CBHW030355290526
45785CB00004B/1761